Time Management

The Book "Unleash Your Full Potential" Is A Hands-on Guide That Will Teach You How To Be More Productive And Make The Most Of Your Time

(The Following Are Ten Helpful Life Hacks That Can Assist You In Being More Organised Focused)

Harry Nunez

TABLE OF CONTENT

Introduction 1

Advantages Of Being Able To Organise Your Time 6

Advice On How To Successfully Complete Household Duties 16

The Top Ten Time Management Mistakes That People Make 37

Avoid Putting Things Off 49

Time Is An Asset That Cannot Be Purchased ... 59

Clear The Clutter From Your Home 91

The Practice Of Zen Rites And Arts 102

Prioritization 111

Why Is Time Management Important? 118

Close Proximity To The Mousepad 133

Individual Who Makes Fun Of Themselves And Says. "I Am In A Very Sedentary State Right Now." 143

Make A List Of Things You Need To Do Every Day. 148

Assessing Productivity While Working To Enhance Our Time Management System 159

Increased Productivity And Achievement Are Obtained 164

What About The Investigations? How Am I Supposed To Establish A Time Limit When There Is So Much For Me To Discover? 172

The Most Effective Practises For Organisation 178

Introduction

We've all had the experience of feeling as if we're "running out of time," and you can definitely remember a moment when you complained that "there aren't enough hours in the day." This is something we've all experienced. It is not a simple job to be able to successfully manage a limited amount of time, and in addition to our own internal procrastinations, there are lots of external distractions that come in the way of our productivity.

In today's fast-paced world, time management is a talent that is difficult to perfect but is highly valued by employers. It is very necessary if you want to be able to complete what you set out to do and, ultimately, if you want to be successful. You may not believe it, but using tactics for smart and successful time management can set you apart from your competition, enable you to do more than they do, and make you more efficient, productive, and lucrative. Without efficient time management, you will discover that hours pass you by in a manner that cannot be retrieved, and you will have nothing to show for the time that was spent working. Time is the most valuable resource that you have.

We all have goals that we'd want to reach, but the question is: how can we make the most efficient use of our time so that we may do as much as we possibly can in the allotted amount of time?

This is a question that I am continuously asking myself since I am someone who is always active in numerous projects at any one moment. In an attempt to discover an answer to this issue and improve my talents, I have meticulously collected ideas at seminars and training sessions where I've learnt from some of the world's best achievers, and I have compiled them into this helpful guide. You can find out more about this in my profile or on my website.

In this article, I will go over everything you need to know to get started increasing the amount of work that you get done in a day. To start, I'll examine why some individuals become unproductive, and although some of the reasons may be obvious to you, others may come as a bit of a surprise. You'll discover that some of the reasons are easy to anticipate, while others may come as a bit of a shock. Time management is not just about managing the timing of your chores, but also managing your energy, and successful time management has an influence not only on your job, but also on areas such as health and fitness. Time management is not only about managing the timing of your tasks, but also managing your energy. I'll go over all of this, and I'll also look at the effect of not making the greatest use of your time, so that you may begin to find ways that will help you build better levels of productivity. I'll speak about all of this, and I'll also look at the impact of not making the best use of your time.

In order to start receiving the outcomes that you truly desire, you will be prepared with not just insights but also practical actions that you can easily execute every day, as well as skills that you can gain simply by altering the method in which you accomplish specific chores. All of this will be provided to you by this book.

Advantages Of Being Able To Organise Your Time

Time is always limited, and the only way to guarantee that you are doing more each day is by controlling the little amount of time you have available to you. There are a lot of individuals who don't think they need to manage their time because they believe that the time they have isn't even enough for them to sit down and plan out how they're going to work on the chores that are in front of them. Managing your time effectively enables you to assume responsibility for the responsibilities that have been delegated to you, allowing you to do more work while still having time for your own personal development and leisure activities. Learning how to manage your time well may enhance a variety of facets of your life. The following is a list of some of the perks that are available to you:

Reduced levels of stress

There are many persons in this world who are affected by stress. Your stress levels may be greatly reduced if you learn to effectively manage your time. The arrival of unwelcome surprises in one's life may be a source of stress; but, given that you will have more time to do more, these unexpected will not stress you out since you will be better able to manage them. Effective time management reduces the number of pressing deadlines to only a few that must be met. There aren't many deadlines that can be completed with little to no tension at all. When you have a solid strategy for your work, you won't have to hurry from one assignment to the next, which is another source of stress. You are not going to continue racing around from one location to another in order to get things done. You are able to finish one activity completely before moving on to the next one if you are working on it in the same area.

It's time to step it up.

There is never enough time in the day to get everything done. This is how you determine how much work you are capable of getting done. Effective time management allows you to do more in the same amount of time. When you make a plan for what needs to be done, you become more aware of the steps you need to take in order to complete the chores on time. Because of this, you now have more spare time to devote to activities that are in addition to the time management list you painstakingly crafted. If you have a lot of work to do and you're not sure how you're going to handle it, planning out how you're going to get it done will show you how simple and quick it is to get things done. Because of this, you are able to do everything in a shorter amount of time.

Leisure time

Everyone has the same number of hours in a day to do the tasks that they are responsible for since time is unchangeable. You may always make better use of your time in order to have some time free at the end of the day to rest, to pamper yourself, and also to spend with key people in your life. However, there is no guarantee that this will happen. To prepare one's body and mind for the next few days, it is necessary for everyone to have some downtime throughout the day, often known as leisure time. This highlights the need of effective time management. You may develop a schedule for everything that has to be done and yet have some time left over for activities that bring you joy and give you the opportunity to unwind.

Reduced exertion

It is a common misconception that in order to work more each day, one must put in a significant amount of effort; however, this is not the case. When you do not have a concrete strategy to complete the duties at hand, you will need to expend more effort. Time management enables one to have a clearer understanding of what they need to do and what is involved in doing so, allowing them to create means by which they may work more quickly with less effort. Time management is intended to simplify your job and save you time. You will be able to save a significant amount of time and effort as a result of the preparation that you do, even if it will take you a few minutes each day to prepare for the next day. You have come to the conclusion that if you have a solid strategy, it will take you less attempts to complete all of the chores.

Almost no blunders

As a result of the lack of a solid strategy, it is difficult for an individual to choose what they should do first and what they should do last; as a result, a lot of individuals begin working on all of the chores at the same time. As a consequence of this, a large number of errors are committed, and as a result, you are needed to do certain duties more than once in the end, which consumes a significant amount of your time and effort. As soon as you begin to manage your time and arrange your activities, all of this will go. When you plan out how you will spend your time in a day, you won't forget some of the things that need to be done. You are going to integrate all of the directions and specifics into the plan so that they will not be forgotten when you are carrying out the plan.

Few challenges to overcome in life

Procrastination, missing critical dates and deadlines, and forgetting about significant events and occasions are the root causes of many of the issues that individuals experience in their lives. Your failure to effectively manage your time will undoubtedly result in all of these plus a great deal more trouble in your life, and you will continue to run into difficulties. If you have a plan for the day and you prepare for all you need to accomplish on that day, you will have less problems to deal with on that day.

Without remorse

When you have a lot of things to accomplish but have wasted a lot of time, you will start to feel regret. People spend their time doing meaningless activities rather than the vital things they should be doing in a day, and then they feel terrible about it at the end of the day. Effective management of one's time may assist one prevent having such regrets. Since you are aware of what has to be done and the amount of time that you have to do it, the likelihood that you will not complete the duties before the end of the day is quite low. Because you already have a strategy, you won't need to spend any more time than necessary attempting to find out what actions you should do next.

A favourable reputation

Most people would rather work with well-organized people who can consistently operate effectively and intelligently. Therefore, effective time management may provide you with fantastic opportunity to work for businesses and employers that appreciate intelligent work rather than large amounts of labour that provide little of value to the organisation. When others are aware of how intelligently you work, it is much simpler to get a decent job or a promotion. People who are able to effectively manage their time also have a reputation for being trustworthy, which is a quality that may open doors to further chances for you in life. Because everyone already knows that they can depend on you for anything, there is no need for anybody to worry about whether or not you will show up for work.

Advice On How To Successfully Complete Household Duties

This is one area in which I have a lot of trouble. When there are tasks that need to be done, the duties around the home are often the least of my concerns. My assumption is that they will still be present when I return to my house. On the other hand, when I come home, I convince myself that I can always complete them the following day. And this continues to be the norm.

Your house is where you go to relax and unwind. It is the gathering spot for all of your loved ones, including your friends and family. When you are organisingyour day, this should be the first thing on your list of priorities. If you have a regular routine for your duties around the home, the place will take care of itself, and you won't have to worry about putting things in order when you find out you have guests coming over.

When it seems as if you don't have any free time in your life, I'm going to offer you some pointers in this chapter on how you may get your duties done around the home even though you're so busy. You are going to be so grateful to me when you aren't scurrying about frantically attempting to tidy your house just before people arrive!

Separate the Pieces

Every time you clean your house, you do not have to clean every square inch of it from top to bottom every time. If that were the case, you would have a full day during which you would be responsible for taking care of your house. I don't know about you, but each day of the week brings with it a new set of tasks and responsibilities for me, many of which include the outdoors. In addition to that, I have a family who would be overjoyed to see me.

As a result, I have devised a method wherein a different section of the house gets cleaned on a daily basis. Everyone in the home is responsible for some aspect of the household chores. For instance, on Monday evenings I concentrate on the living room of the house. As soon as we are all there, we immediately start gathering the necessary cleaning tools and working quickly to finish the space. This might take a longer or shorter amount of time, depending on the number of people living in your home.

When your home has established a reliable schedule, be sure to keep to it.

To win by dividing your opponent's forces.

As I indicated in the last section, breaking up the chores of running a home makes it much simpler to get things done in the allotted amount of time. There are some tasks around the house that must be completed on a regular basis, such as bringing the trash can outside or washing the dishes. Find a method to split these responsibilities among everyone so that everyone has a daily job to do.

When You Get Here, You Need to Get Things Done.

I am the worst person in the history of procrastination. If there's any way I can put it off till later, I definitely would. Having said that, this is a behaviour that has the potential to do a lot of harm and waste a lot of time. Once I get home in the evening, I find it difficult to motivate myself to continue with the rest of my day. How about you? The very first thing that comes to mind is to kick off my shoes and relax on the sofa. When I do this, though, I wind up neglecting the important responsibilities that I have around the home.

When you return home, you should get your tasks done as quickly as you can, and then use the time you had planned to relax to catch up on some sleep. This is the advice I have for you.

Employ Someone to Assist You.

The vast majority of us undoubtedly do not have an abundance of money that would enable us to employ someone to clean our houses for us. On the other hand, if you do, this may be an excellent way to save time. By giving a respectable cleaning business access to your house so that they may clean it, you will not only save yourself the effort of doing the heavy cleaning, but you will also save yourself time.

Maintain a Tidy Appearance

If you give it some thought, you could realise that this is really a time-saving technique. If you are moving through your house and pick up a few items as you go along and put them away, you will save yourself the trouble of doing it later. You were going to have to go in that direction anyhow, so why not put the journey to good use?

Lists of Duties to Perform

This is quite effective when used with youngsters. A weekly duty list that includes both daily and weekly tasks is something that I prefer to hand down to my children. They will get an allowance increase in proportion to how well they execute the tasks. They will not be given an allowance if they do not complete the tasks. It's almost like having a maid service that comes to your house on a regular basis!

Time during which everything will be completed.

It is possible that some activities should not be performed at certain times of the day. Therefore, it is important to have a clear notion of when a work has to be completed and to make it a top priority to complete the assignment at the appropriate time. Dishes cannot be washed until after food has been consumed, and the trash can is not to be emptied until there is anything to be thrown away. Learn the peculiarities of your day and put them into your plan so that everything runs well.

Do whatever it is that gets you through your everyday housekeeping the most efficiently. When you are planning out your day, your home should not be the last thing on your list of priorities. It's possible that you'll be able to put it off until later, but if you do, you could wind up having to clean it for longer than you anticipated. If you include the things that need to be done around the house into the things that need to be done during the day, you will quickly notice that your day is starting to become much more organised.

Do not sit around and wait for things to take place; not only do you need to strike while the iron is hot, but you also need to keep it heated up so that it can become hot in the first place.

When it comes to exercising self-control, this time-tested proverb includes a comma after the last phrase. You won't need an explanation if you've ever had the opportunity to visit the workplace of a blacksmith; you'll just get it. However, even if you haven't been inside one, you should be aware that there is a furnace within that is responsible for heating up the iron.

Heating the metal is required at all times; after it has been properly heated, it will become fluid and may be shaped into a variety of various forms.

The same is true of your life; it's just like the metal in that respect. You can't sit around and do nothing while chances come to you; you have to take action. You must always be on the lookout for new chances and identify the ones that are most suited to you in order to succeed. You can't keep waiting for things to happen, you can't keep making excuses, and you can't keep doing nothing except sitting around watching TV and fantasising about working out.

It is time for you to come to the realisation that you cannot make any more excuses like, "I cannot go for a walk today because I am tired. " If you want to have discipline instilled in you, it is time for you to realise that you cannot make any more excuses like this. I promise that I will go out on another day.

"I will do the assignment at a later time. After that, all I plan to do is watch a movie while I eat something.

Get a jar for your spare change and put it on the counter with the words "Excuse Tax" written on it. Put some money into the pot every time you provide an excuse to yourself—especially one that compels you to act in a certain way—that leads to you acting. It might be one penny, one dollar, one twenty dollar bill, or even one hundred dollar bill.

If you are successful in keeping the jar devoid of anything for a period of three consecutive weeks or 21 days, you are well on your way to achieving redemption.

If you make the decision to do something, then make sure you do it:

A significant number of individuals are susceptible to the pitfall of giving up too readily. When we quit up, things are indeed more difficult, but there is still a potential that if we had continued to become better, we would have been able to handle them. I did discuss going to the gym and how many individuals join fitness centres just after the New Year.

The majority of them just visit for a short period of time in the month of January. After that, they have completely lost interest in going to the gym and never return.

As long as you keep acting in this manner, you will never be able to accomplish what you set out to achieve.

The method is extremely easy to understand and begins with setting expectations that are reasonable. Because we are just discussing a period of 21 days, we won't bother coming up with a complex plan that you have to stick to for a whole year. Let's just say, choose anything that you have been putting off for a while now, and write it down on a piece of paper.

Now that the assignment has been finished, go to the next step and find out what more you may perform during the first 21 days.

If you have chosen a hobby such as learning to play the guitar, beginning an evening stroll every day, purchasing a bicycle and going out on hikes, or any other activity, be sure to write down the ultimate aim of the endeavour. Now, divide the overall objective into more manageable chunks that are each 21 days long, and evaluate your progress.

After you have accomplished that, continue to do the work in the same manner for a period of 21 days and see the results. Invoking your muscle memory is necessary in order to become skilled in a variety of different physical activities. If you are unfamiliar with the concept of muscle memory, you may think about it in the same way as a reflex. A behaviour that you don't even notice but that contributes to the completion of a job automatically.

Remember how difficult it was for you to ride a bicycle when you first started out? You were on the verge of giving up. You are at the point where you no longer even think about how the balance works. You need just push down on the pedals in order to keep the bike from toppling over. This is known as muscle memory, and it is developed over time by repeated use of muscles.

When you finally comprehend how everything is going to play out, you will see that you just cannot give up on the situation. You will find that your capacity for self-discipline improves in direct proportion to the amount of time and effort you devote to developing it. Begin with something simple, then as you gain experience, go on to things that are progressively more difficult to master. You will eventually be able to develop self-discipline, and when you do, you will have a lot of success in completing your work on time and without any interruptions or difficulties.

Step 4: Integrate your plan for the next five years with the plan you have in place right now.

This is the point at which you build your own personal passageway over the vast chasm that we call life. It's possible that without a bridge, you'll spend the rest of your life struggling to make it through difficult circumstances and figuring out how to get out of a maze that never seems to end.

Discover the aspects of your life that are lacking. What steps are you not doing that you should be? In what ways are you failing to make the most of your time? Examine the differences between the two timetables and consider how you may better use key blocks of time in the here and now to achieve your goals and improve your life. Include time spent with family, if that's something you do over the course of the day, in your agenda. Although we have a propensity to assume that we are bound by certain responsibilities in our life, the reality is that this is not the case. We have a responsibility to ourselves, and the value of a human life is determined by the individual living it.

Create a fictitious timetable based on the activities that would most immediately advance you towards the achievement of your five-year goal. Keep in mind that the more steps you take to realise your five-year goal, the more momentum your ship will have as it navigates the limitless chances that we come across during our lives.

The objective is to create the perfect itinerary for this week, as well as for the next three weeks. You are going to put in a little bit of additional effort to make sure that your foundations are sturdy when you are doing a lot of ground work to create the foundation for your house in five years. Your life will become far less stressful after you put these procedures into place.

But before you can just cruise towards your goal, you need to carefully plan out your journey to make sure that nothing goes wrong along the way.

Be careful to build up a monthly timetable for yourself that not only allows you to pay your expenses but also moves you closer to achieving your goals. It is sometimes hard to fit everything into the perfect timetable, but a good example is that if you have to accompany a child to practise, you should have a fun time with your kid on the journey, and then utilise the time spent waiting in the vehicle while practise to take time to work on your goals. Whether you are chronicling the day in your diary, tracking your progress towards your ideal life, or just spending time alone yourself engaging in an activity that you really like, all of these things should have taken place throughout your ideal day.

The Top Ten Time Management Mistakes That People Make

Do you believe you are good at managing your time? The answer, for the vast majority of individuals, is most likely not well. When you are feeling particularly overwhelmed, you may find that the only way to get everything done is to stay at the office much beyond the normal quitting hour, even if your coworkers have already left for the day. Then there may be times when you have one difficulty after another, leading you to be under a significant amount of stress.

The vast majority of us are aware that our current methods of time management leave a lot to be desired, but identifying the specific errors in our practises may be challenging due to the complexity of the situation. On the other hand, when we are successful in managing our time, the rewards become abundantly clear: we experience less stress, and the quality of our work improves.

Let's examine the top 10 most typical errors in time management that we make, as well as the solutions to these problems that we might implement.

In the absence of a To Do List

Do you ever feel as like you've forgotten to do something, and a little voice in the back of your mind reminds you of it? Do you find it stressful when you know you should recall something significant but you just can't seem to put your finger on what it was? If this describes you, then it's likely because you haven't made a list of things that need to be done.

To-do lists are an excellent tool for being organised and on top of things to ensure that time is not wasted in the pursuit of being productive. One useful piece of advice is to prioritise the tasks by placing those that need immediate attention at the head of the list, or to give each activity a number or letter designation (for example, 1, 2, 3, or A, B, C, etc.) so that you can identify the tasks with the highest level of significance.

You may decide to use wider terminology for initiatives that are more extensive; nevertheless, this strategy is often inefficient. For example, if you just write down "Begin Marketing Plan," you could discover that you end up spending time on the tasks you have to do since you haven't provided enough specifics. In circumstances such as these, dividing the tasks at hand up into a greater number of stages (for more information on this topic, see the chapter on Action

Planning) can assist you in better managing your time.

Have you ever been asked where you picture yourself in a year's time, and you were completely unable to answer the question? If you haven't established any personal or professional objectives for yourself yet, now is the perfect moment to do so. When you set objectives, you naturally find yourself organising yourself better; you establish what you need to get there and how to get there. This makes goal-setting an essential component of time management that may help you become more efficient. It's possible that you'll come to the conclusion that some things, as well as certain individuals, aren't worth your time to waste on.

You Don't Make Things a Priority

Putting things in the proper order of importance is necessary for effective time management. If you don't set priorities for yourself, you may discover that you worry about other things, which takes your attention away from the work that you should be performing. As a result, after you have finished your list of things to do, you need to ensure that you have prioritised the activities so that you may do them in the appropriate sequence. It might be challenging to determine which activities are more essential than others at times; however, if you have a better understanding of the differences between them, you will be able to better manage your time.

You Allowed Yourself to Be Interrupted by Distractions.

It is often believed that we squander around two hours every day allowing ourselves to be diverted by things that have no value. Can you even begin to fathom what you may have achieved in that time frame if you had been able to better handle the distractions you faced?

Distractions may take various forms, such as spam or unimportant emails, phone calls, or unscheduled guests, to mention just a few examples; nonetheless, in the end, they all accomplish the same thing: they waste our time. It is consequently in your best interest to understand how you may control your distractions (for more information on distractions, check the chapter before this one). Start getting some work done right away by turning off your Instant Messaging client, putting your phone on vibrate, turning off your Internet connection, and removing any games you may have installed. You'll find that you can get a lot more work done in half the usual amount of time if you just do a few simple things, and I'll show you how to accomplish that below.

The sin of procrastination

The act of putting something off until a later time or date when there is no pressing necessity to do so is an example of procrastination. Putting off doing something when it is not absolutely required might result in feelings of guilt, which can subsequently lead to feelings of stress. You start with feeling guilty because you haven't begun the job, then you start to sense dread, and finally, you get stressed when you strive to do the work on time, or when you fail to finish it on time.

There are a number of helpful tactics available to overcome procrastination, which may be a significant issue for many people. One helpful piece of advice is to promise yourself that you will just work on it for fifteen minutes. Many people who procrastinate do so because they believe they are obligated to do a job in its entirety, which results in emotions of dread and anxiety. However, if you convince yourself that you will just work on it for fifteen minutes, or even for a shorter period of time, you will feel less nervous. Check out the chapter on procrastination for some other helpful hints.

Your Workload Is Too Heavy to Bear

Your coworker just asked for your assistance, stating that she has an urgent need to do something else and asking if you could take over the job that she was working on. Do you always respond "yes" when someone asks for your assistance? It's not easy to turn down requests from friends and coworkers, but there are times when you just have to. There is no use in taking on more work if you are already at capacity in your current job and are struggling to complete your own responsibilities. If you do this, you can notice a decline in the quality of your job, a decrease in your personal drive, and an increase in the amount of stress you feel.

Taking on more work is not a smart practise for time management, and the implications of doing so may prevent you from making success in your career. Master the art of providing a courteous refusal to anybody who could make such a request of you.

Making a living out of "Busy"

There are many who take pleasure in the frenetic pace of life, revelling in the challenge of juggling several commitments at once. However, this may also result in work that is of low quality and a reputation for being unprofessional in the community. You should make an effort to take things slowly and educate yourself on how to better manage your time.

juggling several tasks at once.

When you scratch the surface of the concept of multitasking, though, you may discover that it is not as beneficial as it first seems to be. You might believe that sending an email to your boss while you are on the phone with contractors is an effective way to manage your time, but you might find that you are repeating things that are supposed to go in the email to the contractor, or you might even jot down the conversation that you are having with the contractor in the email that you are sending to your boss. Either way, you might find that you are wasting time. Because of this, your supervisor considers the quality of your job to be subpar, and the contractor considers you to be impolite. After that, you will need to restart the email in order to reduce the impact of the harm that has already been done.

If you want to make the most efficient use of your time, you should avoid multitasking and instead focus on the work at hand. The quality of the job that you do will improve.

You Never Stop for a Refreshment

According to an ancient proverb, a well-fed army is one that marches with confidence. Working until you are so exhausted that you can't stand up straight is not an effective method for managing your time. If you don't take care of yourself, your body won't be able to function correctly, and if it can't function properly, you won't be able to work. Your body requires food, water, and rest. Take frequent breaks, paying careful attention to your time away from the computer. Make time in your schedule for periodic pauses, and don't forget to give your body the fuel it needs.

Not Putting Things on a Schedule To the letter

While some of us are more productive first thing in the morning, others of us prefer to get our work done later in the day. Make an effort to plan specific activities for times of the day when you are positive you will be more productive and have more energy.

Avoid Putting Things Off

Putting things off till later is a dangerous trap that's easy to slip into. What can be accomplished today should not be pushed off until tomorrow. Putting things off till later is a certain way to get into trouble. After you have determined the order in which your chores should be completed, you should immediately go to work on the most pressing and critical ones so that you can get them out of the way. It will be easier for you to keep your attention on the task at hand and complete the job in a timely manner if you begin working on it as soon as possible rather than putting it off. Procrastination is one of the most detrimental things that may happen to your ability to manage your time effectively. You may save yourself a lot of trouble and anxiety in the future if you simply make the decision to complete the assignment and get started on it as soon as you possibly can. I am a great believer that one should get things done as early as possible. When setting priorities, doing the chores that are the most challenging first will free up a lot of time for you to focus on the ones that are easier. If you do not feel inspired to work, one strategy you may try is to write down the things you want to do in the next few hours and then focus your efforts on completing those tasks. When those tasks are finished, you should compile a list of things to do in the next few hours. Working in this manner will make the situation seem less daunting.

Step 6: Don't Get Worked Up Over Irrelevant Particulars

Put your attention where it needs to be, and do not worry about things that are not vital to your success. Stop wasting time and simply get the work done; you'll have plenty of time to go back and make changes afterwards. While you're working, if you let yourself get distracted by petty concerns, you won't go very far. Although you should take care to do the task well the first time around, it is preferable to return to it at a later time and make any necessary adjustments. While working on a job, if you allow yourself to get distracted by the little details, you run the risk of running out of time very fast. Every piece of writing begins with a rough draught, which is then refined in subsequent draughts. Things are seldom perfect the very first time they are attempted. It will end up saving you a lot of time in the long run if you go back and go over the little things afterwards. You will be able to get a lot more work done in a shorter amount of time if you do not let yourself be distracted by trivial concerns that are not in the least bit significant. Don't spend your time trying to be perfect the first time you do anything; simply finish the assignment, look it over, and edit it until all of the fine-tuning is done. simply keep in mind this when you start a new project.

Gain an understanding of habit loops.

In 2006, academic experts came to the conclusion that roughly half of the activities that individuals engage in on a daily basis are not the result of conscious choices but rather are habits.

In one instance, a guy suffered from a very uncommon kind of a virus that led to significant memory loss. Not only had he forgotten how to communicate, but he had nearly completely lost the ability to breathe!

Following a few weeks of therapy, he was able to return to his typical activities, including speaking regularly and doing routine motions. His memory, on the other hand, did not recover.

Even though they gave him their names many times a day, he was unable to recall the names of individuals he often saw. Additionally, he appeared to repeat a lot of his activities, as if he could not remember that he had done them previously.

Nevertheless, there were elements that somehow stayed with him, such as the fact that he knew where in the home to search for food if he needed it. This is due to the fact that these behaviours had transformed into habits as a result of passing through a "habit loop" and were now stored in an entirely other region of the brain.

The trigger, the routine, and the reward are the three components that make up a habit loop. These three components are what contribute to the formation of habits that are sustainable over time.

The cue is analogous to the triggers that we discussed in the earlier part of this discussion in that it is the factor that mechanically communicates to your brain which of the routines stored in your memory must be used. After it follows the routine, which may not always refer to anything that involves movement. It may be a pattern that just exists inside your head, or it might have to do with the way you feel. Both are possibilities.

The prize is the next step after that. This is what enables you to instill a habit more firmly and permanently inside yourself. The reward is another factor that does not have to be anything tangible; it may also be something that has to do with how you feel after accomplishing the goal.

For instance, the gratified and relieved sensation that you experience after successfully completing a challenging activity is an example of anything that might serve as your "reward."

Therefore, if you want to become more productive and develop excellent habits that last, it is vital to establish all three of these processes of the habit loop. If you do this, you will be able to make persistent positive habits.

Now, when it comes to harmful habits, you will need to think about the reward that this terrible behaviour offers you in order to understand how to break the habit. Let's say that one of your terrible habits is to chew your nails first thing in the morning.

It's likely that the fact that, after you've completed this routine, you experience less tension or some other kind of relaxation is the incentive that draws you back to it again and again.

You will need to replace this behaviour with another one that is more beneficial to you and gives you with the same kind of reward in order to break yourself of this habit. You may, for instance, decide to replace one behaviour with another habit, such as the practise of going for a run first thing in the morning. Your body will produce chemicals called endorphins as a result of exercise, and these chemicals will provide a sensation of contentment that is comparable to, or perhaps superior to, the feeling you get from chewing your fingernails or toenails.

Of course, this is but one example among many others. You may use this scenario to help you break any time-wasting habits that you want to get rid of and replace them with behaviours that will serve you better in the long term.

This concludes all you need to know about developing and maintaining productive habits that will assist you in doing more in a shorter amount of time, as well as how to rid yourself of negative triggers that lower productivity and harmful behaviours that waste valuable time.

When striving to successfully manage your time, the next chapter will cover all of the extra information and suggestions that you need to be aware of.

Time Is An Asset That Cannot Be Purchased

The asset of time has a value that exceeds that of monetary wealth. Therefore, do not squander your time. People will build their futures by making productive use of the time that is available to them now. Everyone has the same amount of time, according to God. It is comparable to monetary value. In our world, everything has a price, but time is irreplaceable and cannot be bought or sold. Although money is precious, time is absolutely irreplaceable. Many individuals in the world encourage us to become proficient in time management. Time will cause the sun, the moon, and the earth to rotate about itself. The passage of time brings about a shift in the seasons. They provide us with information on time management and the natural laws. Time, not money, is the most important factor in our lives. Therefore, we must keep up with the passage of time, and maybe, this will impart some significance onto our lives. Time is the essence of both life and greatness. Time is a factor that may influence one's level of success.

Timing is everything when it comes to success. Time moves so quickly. There are going to be some folks in this room who will claim that they don't have time for anything. Those individuals who are not walking or moving in step with the movement automatically are being left behind since they do not have time. Even when we have something as important as time, we nevertheless complain that there is not enough of it because we fritter it away without giving it any thought.

Time was Spent, and Words Were Spoken

The greatest obstacle to achievement is the frittering away of time. When a certain amount of time has passed, it can never be retrieved again. Our cherished present will eventually become the past, which can never be brought back. This adage is accurate in its assertion that time wasted and words said cannot be retrieved after they have been spoken.

We should never put off until tomorrow the tasks that need to be completed today since, if we continue to put off our work until tomorrow and the day after that, it will continue to pile up. Finished work is like fresh food; after it's been done, it loses its appeal. Due to the fact that time is always changing, it is impossible to store it in a static form. We are only entitled to time when we are able to make productive use of it; otherwise, it is just lost. Because our well-being is contingent on how well we manage our time, we need to prioritise it above our financial resources.

Chanakya suggests that a person would always experience failure and regret if they do not pay attention to the passage of time. In spite of the fact that time is both crucial and ever-changing, human history demonstrates that most of the time, we fail to appreciate its actual worth.

IshwarchandraVidyasagar was known to be a prompt and reliable individual. The proprietors of the stores along the alley used to set the time on their clocks based on his appearance. Galileo was a skilled apothecary. By taking time away from his employment, he was able to come up with a large number of discoveries in the scientific world. The anti-slavery book Uncle Tom's Cabin, which was written by Harriet Beecher Stowe despite the fact that she was a busy housewife, received widespread acclaim and is still studied and discussed to this day. The examples shown here indicate that all of these great individuals had one thing in common: they were good at making effective use of their time.

Time is a Predictable Phenomenon in Nature

The study of nature is the most effective way to get an understanding of time management. The passage of time is often seen in a variety of ways, including day and night, variations in temperature, and so on. When there is even the slightest deviation from the norm, the consequences are catastrophic. If we continue to place blame on time, then it will turn a triumph into a loss. Napoleon was able to win the battle against Austria due of a five-minute delay in the army's arrival, but he was captured within a few minutes because his General arrived late. The failure of Napoleon to satisfy the deadlines set for him during the Battle of Waterloo was the primary contributor to his loss. It is claimed that we can earn back the riches that we have lost, and that we can obtain back the knowledge that we have forgotten, but time that has been wasted will never be retrieved, and all that is left for us is regret.

There is great riches in the centre of time, but in order to get it, one must employ time in a strategic manner. The people of Japan serve as a model in this regard. They construct something inventive by using the discarded components of their various toys and little gadgets. They do it in their spare time, and as a result, they make extra income. They experience more joy as a result, in addition to improved time management.

Guru Ramdas was fond of saying that the one who never squanders even a single minute of their lives and always makes the most of the time that they have is the one who is genuinely fortunate.

Time is the rung on the ladder that leads to the summit. The hours and minutes of a day are analogous to bricks, which are used in the construction of a life. Nobody's ever been wealthy or impoverished thanks to Mother Nature; instead, she's given each person an equal share of the richness that comes from having 24 hours in a day. Even if a person is very diligent in their job, it will be for nothing if they are unable to complete their tasks in a timely manner. The crops that were not harvested within the allotted time were thrown away. If you plant your seeds at the incorrect moment, they won't grow. Each passing second in life ushers in brand-new possibilities for a prosperous tomorrow. Who knows, maybe the time we just squandered was intended to bring us good fortune and we simply blew it. We should constantly make the most of every minute that life gives us.

Time is the Creator of Living Things.

It was mentioned by Franklin that one should not squander time since time is the one who creates life. It is not an exaggeration to claim that the proverb "time and tide wait for none" is true. It is our responsibility to make effective use of the time we have.

Time is all we have.

Time is often considered to be synonymous with life. Some people believe that squandering time is the same as wasting one's life, and vice versa. If you use your time carefully, then the quality of your life will be much improved.

Once upon a time, a holy man posed the following question to his followers: "What is the most important thing in life that should neither be lost nor be misused, because even God cannot bring it back?" All of the disciples agreed that money, love, parents, family, patience, bravery, power, knowledge, faith, a teacher, God, and breath were the most important things in their lives.

His most trusted student gave the correct response, which was that the answer was "time," explaining that everything else, with the exception of breath, may be regained after being lost, but that we eventually have to quit taking breaths. Therefore, time is the one and only commodity in life that should never be wasted since it can never be gained again.

The downfalls of juggling many tasks at once

In spite of the many benefits and advantages detailed above, one must remember that multitasking also comes with a few drawbacks that they must avoid at all costs. Let's take a look at a few of these negative aspects.

When you transfer from one activity to another when multitasking, you lose a significant amount of time in the transition. Multitasking results in a significant loss of time. Even the most experienced multitaskers are susceptible to this loss of efficiency. According to studies, the human brain operates much like a computer.

When we go from working at one job to working at another, it is analogous to delivering a command to the computer to exit one application and launch another one. According to a number of different scientific studies and polls, the amount of time that passes before our brains are able to produce efficient results while switching jobs is around fifteen minutes on average. This is true even if both may be opened at the same time.

If you are going to transition between tasks right through the day, you may calculate the total amount of time that will be wasted. Therefore, there is no question that attempting to multitask at the same time wastes a considerable amount of time.

It takes a significant amount of energy to multitask, and when we get up, we all have a certain amount of energy available to us. As the day goes, this source of energy becomes more exhausted since each of our everyday chores drains energy from it. When you multitask, it takes more time and energy since you have to transition your body and mind from one activity to another more often.

It requires effort to reconfigure your system so that you can concentrate on the new work, to adjust the demands of your body and mind so that they are in line with the specifications of the new activity, and so on. Also, when you are attempting to accomplish numerous tasks at the same time, you are likely to feel frustrated as you attempt to balance all of the work that needs to be done. Keeping this fury under control also demands a lot of energy.

Compare this to a scenario in which your system is only devoted to the completion of a single task. Your energy reserve is being depleted, yet it is only being utilised for one activity totally. There is no loss as a result of the energy being dispersed among a number of different sites. Because this strategy saves energy, you will be able to do more with the same amount of resources.

Loss of some interpersonal skills is a consequence of multitasking since, in today's technologically advanced world, practically all contacts must take place digitally, such as by email, text message, and other forms of electronic communication. The quality of our abilities to interact with one another has suffered as a direct consequence of our over reliance on modern technologies.

The demands that humans have in their social lives cannot be met by the current state of technology. It is essential for us to engage in conversation with other people. Picking up the phone and talking to someone face-to-face may often produce outcomes that are impossible to achieve via communication channels such as email or chat. You cannot expect to get the same outcomes by communicating just via electronic means such as email and text message.

As a consequence, engaging in an excessive amount of multitasking might cause you to feel lonely, despite the fact that there are people all around you. This feeling of isolation may lead to feelings of loneliness, melancholy, and hopelessness, all of which can have a detrimental effect on a person's mental health.

When your mind is focused on numerous things at the same time, it is easy to get confused about the amount of time and effort that is required to finish tasks. This may lead to procrastination. Multitasking fosters a procrastinating mindset. In addition, the fact that you are successful in doing a number of tasks concurrently gives you an erroneous feeling of self-assurance, and you find yourself thinking along the following lines:

Tomorrow, in addition to the other, more straightforward assignment, I will finish this one.

That task is not nearly as significant as this one.

Due to the fact that I only have 15 minutes left before lunch, I will need to combine this task with the other two that I have scheduled to do in the afternoon.

An attitude of procrastination is fostered by the condition of perplexity and overconfidence that characterises it. We start to believe that putting off our job will not be a significant issue since we are able to multitask and do two or three chores at the same time. Because of our inflated feeling of self-assurance, we tend to forget that juggling many tasks simultaneously requires both more time and more effort than focusing on a single activity. Given the circumstances, it is probable that we may be late for our own deadlines as well.

Why does anything like this occur? The mental and physical exhaustion that comes along with trying to multitask is the major cause of procrastination that it brings about. Keep in mind that completing one item at a time requires far less effort and time than attempting to multitask. The problem is that you don't even realise it until you feel the exhaustion of your body and mind as a result of unfavourable results such as missing deadlines, putting off work, and other such things. A decrease in efficacy and productivity is the direct outcome of mental weariness brought on by excessive multitasking.

You won't be able to get the most essential things done because you're trying to juggle too many things at once. Almost every form of activity that involves multitasking concentrates on the most basic parts of various tasks and endeavours. This occurs when our minds get preoccupied with the idea of completing a greater quantity of tasks rather than concentrating on the significance of the quality of the job that should be prioritised.

In the end, we tend to place more importance on how effortlessly we can finish tasks as opposed to how far we are willing to go to ensure that vital things are taken care of. When we do a lot of little tasks, we give ourselves a phoney sensation of achievement.

The difficulty with having this mentality is that important tasks is neglected as a result. Because of this, our minds are persuaded to believe that we have achieved a great deal, while in fact we have not even come close to doing anything of genuine significance.

Make it a habit to...

The easiest option, chaos does not lead to the most desirable outcomes. It is tempting to carry out random chores at random times throughout the day when the need arises; nevertheless, doing so is not encouraged since it may lead to confusion and inefficiency.

In the long term, you will be rewarded for the methodical way in which you allocate different duties to different periods of the day. In order to build habits, you need to make it a point to do particular activities at regular times throughout each day. This may not always be possible to do due to the fact that you may be confronted with a wide variety of unexpected occurrences at your place of employment or when you are managing your company, both of which need your immediate attention.

In spite of the fact that you were meant to be doing your daily simulation tests from ten in the morning until twelve in the afternoon, as you have been doing for the last several days, you could end yourself talking to someone on the shop floor about an issue instead. Despite this, you should still make it a priority to develop good behaviours. The process of dividing up work into discrete chunks of time, often known as "time boxing," is an excellent strategy for boosting productivity while simultaneously cutting down on time-consuming inefficiencies.

The act of checking e-mail, engaging in creative thinking or financial planning, as well as participating in meetings or conference calls, are all examples of habits.

In addition, if you plan to carry out comparable activities at certain time intervals but yet maintain some degree of flexibility, you might think about what the action you are now engaged in is attempting to accomplish. For instance, you may divide activities up into the following categories, and then carry them out at various points during the day:

Assign responsibilities: Participate in meetings and conference calls, as well as delegate tasks to independent contractors, full-time workers, and freelancers.

Enhance both the procedures and the products: Increasing the speed at which the assembly line works, cutting down on waste, doing away with or combining certain activities, cutting down on the number of components used in the assemblies, providing high-quality training to staff, ensuring the healthy development of the business or firm, and looking for methods to advertise more effectively

Reduce the number of flaws in the product or service, mediate any conflicts that arise amongst personnel, and provide solutions to issues relating to communication, operation, and the budget.

You should make use of a to-do list if you often fail to meet deadlines, have feelings of being overburdened by the amount of work you need to do, or even sometimes forget to carry out essential responsibilities. A "to-do list" is a piece of paper or a sheet of paper that has a list of chores that you need to do, organised in the order of their importance to you. This indicates that the most essential chores are located at the front of the list, while the tasks with a lower priority are located towards the list's bottom. Having this sort of list may assist guarantee that all of your significant responsibilities are addressed to in a timely manner and that you do not neglect to complete the chores that are stated.

When you utilise a to-do list, you not only get to alleviate the burden of an excessive amount of work, but you also establish a reputation for being dependable, organised, focused, and highly productive in what you do. You will get the impression that there is nothing to worry about since all of your work for the day is over and there is no sign of tension. Because you offer your best effort to the activities that are most essential, you will become more useful to your employer and more productive as a consequence of prioritising your job. When you have the greatest energy, you should focus on completing these things first.

Making a list of things you need to accomplish is not enough; in order to advance your career via increased productivity, you need to utilise those lists effectively, organise them in the right way, and come up with a list of tasks that has been well considered.

A. Instructions for Making a To-Do List

To begin, you have the option of either downloading a free template for a to-do list or getting a pen and some paper ready. After that, carry out the following steps:

Determine the activities that you are tasked with doing within the confines of the given day. Keep in mind that major jobs should be broken down into smaller actions or tasks that are simpler to do.

Establish a hierarchy for the tasks by placing the most important ones at the front of the list (these might also be the tasks with the highest priority), and the tasks with a lower priority at the bottom of the list. In the event that a large number of jobs are rated as having a high priority, you will need to reorganise them according to which ones need urgent attention. For instance, activities that have limited amounts of time to complete them might be prioritised for immediate action.

B. Putting Your To-Do List to Work for You

You need to begin working from the top of the list down, beginning with the jobs that are most urgent. To prevent any mistake, jobs that have been finished should be crossed off the list or marked with a checkmark to indicate that they are done. The most effective and convenient to use are brief lists that have been compiled for everyday consumption. On the other hand, if you have significant responsibilities that rely on the efforts of other people, you should think about compiling a long-term list and dividing it up into manageable chunks that can be completed on a daily basis. You should set aside around ten minutes every evening to compose your to-do list; this is a list that will be utilised the following day.

Making Use of Software

In addition to using paper-based lists, you may also utilise software to automate your list of things that need to be done. Even though you will require training to understand how the programme works, it is quite effective. They may be synchronised with emails and phones, and if you are working with a group on a project, you can quickly share your to-do list with the other members of the group. They also include reminders that will warn you when the deadlines for particular activities that have not been completed are drawing near. The ability to simply update your list by swiftly reorganising tasks and setting priorities is one of the advantages of utilising a software programme that manages your to-do list.

The following are some of the tools, among many more, that I recommend:

Please keep in mind the Milk ToodledoTodoist.

Todoist is a helpful app that I use on a regular basis since it fits my needs. It does not cost anything, it is really simple to use, and the design makes it so there are no distractions. You are, of course, free to choose a different instrument. This is only a suggestion based on what has worked successfully for me in the past. It is essential that you identify the instrument that is providing you with the most beneficial outcomes.

Before deciding on a tool, it is vital to do some study since the functions performed by various pieces of software are not the same, and neither are people's neurological make-ups. This guarantees that you will choose a tool that is suitable for your needs. As long as you are satisfied with whatever you choose to utilise, it doesn't matter what it is.

With the help of to-do lists, you can ensure that you complete and remain on top of all of your significant choices and chores.

Clear The Clutter From Your Home.

The full process of decluttering your home might take several days or perhaps a week, which is more time than you have available right now. Follow through with a strategy and commit to spending two hours every day clearing a small section of your house, such as a single bookshelf, the space under the bed, a closet or a wall in the garage. Your mental energy and motivation to finish the full assignment will rise if you first break down a large work into smaller parts and then accomplish each of those sections in turn.

Various Suggestions for Cleaning Out Every Room Kitchen

Consider getting rid of any duplicates or additional items after going through all of your kitchenware such as your pots, cutlery, and plates. Items that you don't use on a regular basis should be given to someone else or passed on to someone else. To better organise the rest of the goods in your kitchen, use the same procedure with them all.

Match up the objects in your plastic ware in descending order from highest to lowest. Make sure you have a well-organized space to store things in so that you can quickly find parts that match when you need them. Don't keep any parts that don't go together.

If you do not have an urgent purpose for whipped cream, plastic butter, or other similar items, you should avoid storing them in your home.

To construct shelves in your cabinet or pantry specifically for storing canned goods, you may use tiny pieces of wood. Put the newest things at the rear and the oldest things in the front.

Examine the contents of your refrigerator and pantry to compile a shopping list before venturing out to the supermarket. Stick to the items on the list.

Place products in the refrigerator that can be seen inside of clear plastic or glass containers. This will ensure that your family is aware of the meals that are currently accessible.

Replace cumbersome boxes of cereal or pasta with airtight plastic containers that can be stacked more easily and are more convenient to store.

The loo

Make the most of the space in the drawers by using dividers or little baskets of various sizes. Sort the objects according to their applications. For instance, goods for oral hygiene may go into one basket, while those for personal grooming could go into another.

If you want to save money and avoid purchasing more products, arrange spare bottles of shampoo and other personal items in an organised form on a shelf.

Plastic milk crates may be used to construct additional storage areas as well as shelves inside of larger cabinets.

Purchase a little container or caddy for each individual living in your home. They may store their own razor, shampoo, conditioner, and other shower essentials in the caddy, and then retrieve it when it is time to take a shower. The accumulation of a dozen bottles in the bathtub may be avoided by using individual containers.

Instead of storing aesthetic pieces that serve no practical use, you should make use of the area that is designated for storage to keep essential objects.

The bedrooms

It is best not to store anything beneath the bed, since this is a common location for the accumulation of dust and other particles. If you need to store things, shallow plastic tubs are a good option for doing so. This is a fantastic method for storing clothes appropriate for the many seasons.

Never, ever leave clothes on the bed or hung over any piece of furniture. For objects that are soiled, you should use a basket or a hamper.

As soon as you wake up, you should make your bed. Your bedroom's appearance will be improved immediately, and you'll be more inspired to keep it tidy as a result.

Invest in dressers of an acceptable size for your wardrobe and steer clear of packing them to capacity at all times. Get rid of any articles of clothing that you haven't worn in the last year.

The Living Area in Addition to the Dining Room

It is possible that unneeded goods will begin to accumulate in any flat space in your living area; thus, you should resist the temptation of flat areas.

Invest 10 minutes of your time every day on clearing the clutter off the floor, sofa, coffee tables, dining tables, and end tables in the living room.

Invest in a box or a wicker basket of suitable size for each member of the family. They should be labelled and kept in a separate area. Every day, go through your dining and living areas and put away any objects that belong in the corresponding basket. It is up to each individual member of your family to ensure that their personal belongings are returned to the correct location.

Be cautious when adding ornamental components since there is a delicate line between adding aesthetic value and creating clutter. If any of your accents are interfering with your ability to go about your daily life, you should either move them or get rid of them.

You should always clear the dining table and wipe it off after each meal. Continually contributing to the mess on the table by leaving objects that aren't being utilised or dishes that are too tiny to use.

The garage

Installing shelves along at least one wall of the garage is a great way to keep debris off the floor and out of sight.

Avoid putting anything you want to keep in storage in the cardboard boxes. To store objects in a manner that is more organised, you may use bins with labels or transparent plastic boxes.

Mount hooks on the wall or install pegs in the ceiling to hang tools, bicycles, or other sports equipment.

Installing a mesh sports hammock in one of the corners will allow you to keep balls and other objects of a similar size.

Both the Basement and the Attic

Construct shelves along the wall and store things in plastic bins placed on the shelves.

Give each individual their own part of the attic or basement to store their belongings, and provide them with a container that is clearly labelled.

Set aside one day every six months for the whole family to go through the basement and attic together, sorting through the belongings to decide what should be kept and what should be discarded.

Store products that are often used at the front or in an area that is easily accessible. Items that are used less often or just during certain times of the year should be kept towards the rear, top, or bottom of the storage rooms.

Utilise the walls and ceilings of the space for hanging objects to store them.

Storage Areas

You should get rid of everything that you haven't utilised in the last year.

When storing shoes or other tiny objects, use bag storage or racks that dangle from the ceiling.

To limit the amount of storage space that you need, utilise vacuum-seal bags wherever it is practicable to do so.

Try to avoid putting things straight on the floor of your closet while you're storing things. To get a higher level of organisation, you may install more shelves or use plastic containers.

The Practice Of Zen Rites And Arts

It is much easier to be productive when both your body and mind have had a chance to get some rest. If you have a lot of work to do, the morning is the best time to do it since that is when you will be the most productive. If you have a lot of work to do, the morning is the best time to do it. Nevertheless, what are your plans for the remaining hours of the day? For many people, this means playing catch-up and attempting to stay on top of their inbox, phone, and email messages while still attending meetings and carrying out any other responsibilities that have been assigned to them. Those who believe this are, sadly, mistaken in their assumptions about the situation. It's not surprising that you're unable to fit anything into your schedule if you go about your day in such a disorganised manner; you just don't make the time for anything. You are so busy trying to make everyone happy that you are unable to effectively shut people down and get anything done. Because you are never at your workstation, the number of items in the in basket continues to increase. You spend too much time performing meaningless activities that do not advance your situation.

Zen

The Chinese have developed a brilliant method of getting rid of clutter, which is applicable to both your day-to-day existence and your overall success in life. They clean up the mess that they made. They are the ones that know where everything is, and this is the first thing that you need to do. Your level of productivity will increase after you have everything in its proper location and are aware of where everything is. You won't have to spend time hunting for a certain file in the system. You are familiar with the location of your pen and pad, and you are able to take meticulous notes to remind you of the activities you have scheduled for the day as well as the things that you need to remember to take notes about.

The practise of Zen also involves emptying one's thoughts. Meditation is something that, if you've never tried it before, may assist you in organising all of the thoughts and ideas floating about in your mind. Imagine the inside of your mind to be the same as the inside of your house or your workplace. For it to operate at its full potential, it requires some amount of organisation. How exactly does one cleanse their thoughts via the practise of Zen?

One of the finest things you can do is to make meditation a regular part of your life. You can argue that you don't have enough time for it, but trust me when I say that you really don't have enough time to avoid using it. By putting your mind's ideas, which have been disorganised during the day, back where they belong, meditation makes it possible for your mind to process more information rather than less. Meditation helps the mind attain the levels of focus that it needs to be successful. Whether you practise walking meditation before a board meeting or silent meditation in the evening to help you sleep better, both are beneficial and make excellent use of your time. Meditation offers the mind the concentration levels that it needs to be successful.

It invigorates, and when you are invigorated, you have a greater tendency to do more. Consider it in this light: if your head is free of mental clutter, you will be able to do tasks without being easily distracted. You are able to complete the work at hand without being interrupted and a great deal more quickly than you would have been able to accomplish it otherwise. The reason for this is because you have not allowed anything to stand in your way. It is highly recommended that you enrol in some lessons if at all possible since doing so is the most efficient technique to clear the clutter from your thoughts.

The effects that meditation has

Before you write off the concept as absurd, you should know that practising meditation does not need you to go into uncomfortable postures. It's not about yelling slogans at the top of your lungs and making a show of yourself. Emptying the mind of all ideas and allowing the energy inside you to become highly balanced are both necessary steps in this process. Because of this, you are better able to maintain your composure in the face of whatever challenges may be thrown your way. It entails training oneself to breathe in the appropriate manner and focusing one's attention only on perfecting that breathing technique. Meditation is known to have a positive impact on mental health in addition to the positive effects it has on one's physical health. You provide vitality. You are able to do more since you are not wasting time overthinking things.

You may acquire a better sense of equilibrium via meditation. It's almost like placing all of the concepts in their appropriate containers, and then being able to come up with new ideas and new thoughts as a result. This enables you to concentrate on the activity that you consider to be the most essential of all of them and do it successfully. It's possible that meeting a target completion time for a project will be the most essential thing you have to do today. Following your meditation session, you will begin the task at hand, during which you will ensure that you are not disturbed in any way, and you will continue to work on it until it is completed. That is the simplest way to put it. You will most likely have a list of things that need to be done, and although lists in and of itself are not unhealthy, prioritising your tasks is. Examine the list once it has been compiled. Make a decision on what you are going to do, and check that box. After that, you must put an end to all other forms of communication and distraction and concentrate on achieving that objective.

In today's world, it is common practise for individuals to let various distractions to prevent them from being productive. What you are seeing is what you may open up for yourself after a session of meditation or first thing in the morning. Imagine the days before email, before mobile phones, and before all of the distractions of social media. This presents a chance to do the seemingly impossible. Before I started using the List and Do approach that I use today, I was under the constant pressure of meeting impossible deadlines, which caused me a lot of stress. Not only do I never miss a deadline, but I also never allow anybody else's activities to impede the progress I've made towards my goals. I have a social life, but I control when I make myself accessible to other people, and that's part of the challenge. The second component is being aware of when your energy levels are low and filling your mind with a enough amount of meditation in order to re-energize the mind so that it can handle the next job that has to be completed.

Prioritization

You are aware of the sinking sensation that you get when you have a lot of things to do, right? When you make an effort to organise your tasks according to priority, but it insists that everything be treated as equally important, what do you do? It is a challenge that everyone will inevitably encounter at some point, so try not to let yourself get overwhelmed by it. Despite the fact that it is difficult to deftly balance several requirements and competing duties, it is not impossible. Prioritisation is a process that involves evaluating a collection of objects and placing them in the order of relevance. As a general rule, prioritisation means doing "first things first;" as a technique, it means doing "first things first."

Keeping a Healthy Balance Between All of Your Tasks

Both Planning and Prioritisation are essential parts of every successful endeavour. Planning entails giving some thought to the activities that must be completed in order to achieve the goal that is being pursued. When you prioritise, you make sure you are working on the most important projects first. The ability to prioritise tasks and plan ahead is one of the most valuable skills a supervisor can possess. They ensure that your efforts, as well as the efforts of your group, are used effectively.

Maintaining Command of the Situation!

1. Determine the goals to be accomplished within the allotted amount of time.

2. Construct a plan to follow in order to achieve those goals.

3. Establish a daily agenda and routine for yourself to follow.

4. To avoid the common blunders and traps that are inherent in the management of time, use strategies for time administration.

The process of making the most efficient use of limited time and resources in the face of an overwhelming number of competing demands is known as prioritisation. Every every day, a boss will be inundated with demands that have the word "IMMEDIATELY" written on top of them. Demands for meetings that never stop, day-to-day reports that are always the same, pressing agent difficulties, and urgent errands to do — and so on and so forth — the list goes on and on forever and ever! If you allow yourself to become caught up in the never-ending cycle of trying to juggle too many things at once, you will inevitably finish up worn out, frustrated, and furious.

Making a Checklist of Things to Do

It goes without saying that you must an ideal strategy that enables you to do everything within the allotted amount of time in order to effectively manage both your time and your finances. In conclusion, you really need to have a foolproof strategy. You could do anything with a simple to-do list.

Those days when there are a million things to accomplish and we don't even know how we're going to do it all are something that we all go through at some point. It is not at all difficult to get overwhelmed by the never-ending quantity of duties that we are expected to do from day to day. When we have a lot of balls in the air at once, it's easy to lose track of the little things that still need to be taken care of and overlook opportunities that might have a significant impact on our lives. When we have an excessive amount of work to do, we start to feel as if we are unable to keep our heads above water. This sensation lasts as long as the excessive amount of work continues.

If we had been more organised and maintained a more stable position, none of this would have been a possibility. In circumstances of this kind, when time is of the essence and stress levels are high, the use of a to-do list is going to be your best bet. It is recommended that you write down all that you need to do in a given day on a list. Just keep it straightforward: jot down the information and the calculations that you need to do, and have that list with you at all times. Keeping it on your person will be of tremendous assistance to you since it will always be in front of you, serving as a reminder to complete the duties in accordance with the allotted amount of time.

You may make sure that you don't forget anything important by maintaining a list like this, which will guarantee that all of your tasks are written down in a one location. In addition, when you organise your assignments, you also set the order in which you will complete them, with the purpose of being able to distinguish between tasks that need your immediate attention and those that can be postponed until a later time.

Make a note of the bulk of the tasks that you are responsible for completing.

Walk through these activities and assign demands on a scale from A (important or very crucial) to F (irrelevant or not in the least bit sincere).

To-Do Lists may be of aid to you in getting on top of important tasks and a large number of errands or decisions, as well as in maintaining that status.

Why Is Time Management Important?

People often think of time management as a productivity tool that may help them get more done in a shorter amount of time. Nevertheless, effective time management is capable of much more than this.

A life that is more balanced and satisfying may be achieved by effective management of one's time, which allows one to regain control of one's life, establish objectives, and meet targets.

A lot of individuals are under the impression that they will never achieve their objectives. They believe it is difficult for them to have a happy life, go to exotic locations, find a job of their dreams, finish things on time, get enough sleep, and make time for their friends and family. They claim that they need more than twenty-four hours to do all of this job. The next step is for them to give up on the concept of pursuing the life of their dreams after having this thinking.

If you are serious about getting your life in order, reading the following chapters will help you comprehend how you may initiate the utilisation of time in your own life. You will be able to master this enchanted ability with the assistance of this book, and so bring about positive change in your life.

Use your Ingenuity to Win!

It allows you to do more in the same amount of time. This is by far the most popular explanation for why individuals desire to learn how to better manage their time. If you are able to successfully manage your time, you will be able to do a great deal more in a given day, week, month, or year.

It assists you in establishing objectives and achieving those goals. Managing your time well is not only about completing more tasks. In addition to this, it is about attaining the objectives that you set for yourself. If you can improve your ability to manage your time, you will be able to improve your ability to create objectives and more easily attain those goals.

It enables you to lead a life that is more well-rounded. Productivity is just one aspect of effective time management. It's also about finding the right balance. If you are able to understand how to manage your time, you will be able to bring more equilibrium into your life and make time for the things that are important to you in addition to the things that are urgent.

It aids in the alleviation of anxiety. Time management is beneficial for a number of reasons, but one of the most important reasons is that it may help alleviate anxiety. The effective management of time is the best antidote to stress there is. If you are able to efficiently manage your time, you will always be able to maintain your composure and serenity no matter what the circumstances are. Put all your worries behind you and focus on having as much fun as possible. But keep in mind that the point of life is to enjoy yourself while being self-controlled. If you put some thought into it, it will shower you with an abundance of love and moments filled with joy.

In addition to these benefits, it may also help you develop into a person who is goal-oriented and is prepared to live an organised and joyful life. Time management may also help you learn about yourself, which is information that will be useful to you for the rest of your life.

Delegation and outsourcing make up Strategy No. 4

Intelligent individuals tend to be entrepreneurs. I concur. They are skilled in a variety of areas. They are juggling a number of different problems simultaneously regardless of the size of the company that they are operating.

Putting together a new business is a simple endeavour. It is open to everyone to do. More than just skill, creativity, money, and experience are required to launch and maintain a successful company brand. It involves a lot of effort, perseverance, and thoughtfulness on your part. Your contribution, as well as the contributions of the other members of your team, should be considered an effort. You cannot be solely responsible for running your company. This is something that every excellent leader is aware of.

People with vision make for excellent leaders. They came here in order to clear a way. Instruct the members of your team on how to properly carry out a business technique. You should delegate the remaining tasks to your management and employees. Doing the most essential job is your responsibility as the boss of the company, a freelancer, or an entrepreneur.

Recruiting skilled individuals to participate on the platform should be your top priority. Allow them to develop together with your company. When it comes to hiring specialists, small businesses just do not have the financial resources. The World Wide Web has helped us do these duties more quickly and efficiently. You may get started working with a virtual assistant for as low as $5 per hour right now.

The process of outsourcing has never been simpler or more cost-effective. Freelancers seem to have an incredible lifestyle, judging on what I've observed. At first, students are responsible for all of the job individually. They put forth a lot of effort to establish a reputable brand. After that, they outsource the company operations by recruiting workers from all around the world.

In the past, I used the services of a virtual assistant who was in charge of monitoring my inbox and sending out emails on my behalf. That wonderful chap shaved three to four hours off my weekly work schedule. If I checked my inbox once per hour instead of spending that time with my family, I would feel much more fulfilled.

The idea of "digital managers" first came to my attention over a year ago. These managers contribute to the work done in my workplace by using Skype. They have a camera set up, so they are able to keep an eye on everything that goes on in the company. At the conclusion of the day, my digital manager gave me a brief report that outlined the day's activities. Employing a digital manager is going to save you a significant amount of money compared to hiring someone to work in your office.

Gains to Be Obtained Through Outsourcing

1. The preservation of both time and money

2. An endeavour

3. Concerns over the cost of training and available labour

4. Expenses related to operations

5. The ability to control one's own time and place

You may be able to outsource a limitless amount of jobs, depending on the nature of your company.

I'm going to go over a few of the responsibilities that you may delegate to others in order to reclaim some of your valuable time.

This is the list that we have:

1. Finance and Accounting 2. Financial Services 3. Management of Social Media

4. Management of databases 5. Web-based application development 6. Internet-based marketing

7. Composing Texts and Editing Them

8. Exercise of self-control 9. Paying taxes 10. Performing administrative duties

11. Advertising 12. Internet search engine

13. Training for salespeople 14. Writing and management of blogs

15. Administration of payrolls 16. Administration of human resources

17. Management of the Work Schedule 18. Doing the Laundry and Shopping 19. Translation and Transcription

20. Visual and Aural Content Related activities

You are better able to concentrate on "generating income" when you outsource. As the owner of the company, it is your responsibility to bring in revenue. You decided to create a company so that you could increase your income. Take care of one particular task and delegate the others.

Find Yourself a Competent Contractor.

You are unable to take a step back until you have recruited the most qualified individual for the role at hand. The success of your company is heavily dependent on your ability to locate the ideal partner. In this respect, online employment portals might be of use to you. Checking in on your social networks should be the first thing you do, in my opinion.

Inquire with your supervisors as to whether or not they know someone who can provide the necessary business services. Make an effort to contact other employers in business and inquire for a referral from them. The networks on LinkedIn and Twitter might also be of use to you.

You may hire specialists for anything from $5 and $100 per hour. It is dependent on the finances of the firm as well as the positions that are involved. Set up an online interview with the applicants who were selected for further consideration. Before employing someone, make sure they have a solid portfolio.

The next stage of the recruiting process is management.

Building trust between you and the freelancer is going to be necessary. Demonstrate to them that you not only have the financial means, but also need high-quality services. The escrow system is used by online job marketplaces such as Freelancer.com, Odesk, and Elance to ensure the security of its users' financial transactions. You may get professional assistance from these websites at an early stage of the process.

Close Proximity To The Mousepad

Keeping your clipboard and pencil next to your mouse cushion is an efficient way to cut down on the amount of time you spend writing. If you ever need to quickly record anything, you have the ability to do it at your fingertips.

If you want to record something, don't make it difficult for yourself by placing it on a whiteboard across the room or requiring that you open a note pad or something to that effect. Personally, I prefer to write on a single list card because it doesn't take up an excessive amount of space. However, the fact of the matter is that if you want to record something, you shouldn't make it a problem for yourself. Make sure the device you use to write is near to your computer.

The Reasons Behind My "Shred Happy" Attitude Towards Notes

If you were to take a look at one of my note pads, you would see that many of the pages are missing. There are several words and lines that have been erased. Why? I abhor unnecessary muddle!

My brain is only capable of storing a certain amount of information at one time, and I don't want it to store an excessive amount of ideas because I want to be able to concentrate without being distracted. Additionally, it is essential to get rid of "flash" thoughts, which the notebook helps me achieve.

Attending a workshop or participating in a teleseminar call exposes you to information that you are only somewhat acquainted with. It is not difficult to get energised and capture everything that every single person says. In point of fact, you are only going to be required to record no more than ten percent or less of what they say, and you will only end up acting on one percent or less of anything that people really say to you. You need to filter through anything that other people tell you that does not speak to your own strengths, even if there is really nothing negative that can be said about it.

Research on people's ability to remember things like street addresses, phone numbers, and counting systems has shown that most people can only keep three or four items in their heads at once. Do you think it's a coincidence that telephone numbers are broken up into groups of three or four digits, rather than groups of seven or eleven? What are some possible observations about the huge numbers separator? You don't write "5000000"; rather, you write "5,000,000."

My conscious brain is capable of monitoring three to four different things at once. I really need to get rid of as many ideas as I can from my notes and only concentrate on the few activities that would bring in the most money for me right now. I will do this so that I can concentrate more clearly.

In the end, we were all successful in achieving "sparkles." You could overhear a statement made on the heat of the moment that leads you to contemplate something far more interesting. At this point, you can scarcely wait to put idea into action or elaborate on it. During a presentation, jot down some notes in your notebook. On the flight home, look over those notes and strike through everything that was relevant while you were thrilled but isn't relevant now that you've had time to collect your thoughts.

Because of this, I mark vast amounts of notes with a cross and destroy old pages that I don't need to deal with: I have to get rid of the glitter, destroy the confused knowledge that I will never use, and simply concentrate on as few ideas as I can.

13th Efficient Way to Save Time: Touch Typing

If you are not using this next skill, then something is amiss with you, and you really need to have this fixed as soon as possible. This next ability is most likely the most effective tool there is.

Acquire the skill of typing from memory. Not only will you achieve all the more, but assuming you work at a normal everyday employment, you will be significantly more attractive because that is another thing you can list on your resume. However, if you are unable to type from memory, then what are you doing with your life?

You are going through the motions of searching and pecking while simultaneously having a look at the console. If you can type from memory and have learned the home column, you can look at your screen to check your progress. The more you practise, the fewer errors you will make, and the faster you will really want to type. If you can type from memory and have learned the home column, you can look at your screen.

The best software for this is "Mavis Beacon Teaches Typing," and I am aware of others that advise correspondence software like "Mythical Beast NaturallySpeaking," but so far I haven't had much success with either of them. The best software for this is "Mavis Beacon Teaches Typing." For the tasks I'm using it for, nothing has been more useful than the ability to contact type.

14th Efficient Way to Save Time: Auto Save

The next step is to back up your work periodically and, if at all possible, set it to save automatically. I am aware that certain products, like Microsoft Word, have an automatic saving function. I am aware that the software for mind mapping that I am using for this video, which goes by the name "FreeMind" and is completely free, also saves automatically. There is one problem with the programming of the auto save feature, and that is the fact that when you create another archive, the programme will not do an auto save until the archive has a record name.

You have the option of opening yet another Word report, typing two or three pages into it, and leaving it as an unnamed or unsaved report, or anything to that effect. Save your work when you have around two or three minutes worth of material, and make it a habit to continue to use "Ctrl-S" every few minutes after that. In this way, even if the power goes out, your computer has an accident, or you accidentally shut the window, you've only missed two or three minutes of work, which isn't a huge amount of time considering everything else that might have happened.

You could be thinking to yourself, "If I save my work frequently, this won't amount to one moment per day," but I'm here to tell you, "Contrary." What if your computer only had a minor malfunction once a month, or if you only misplaced one report every single month due to an unforeseen circumstance?

That indicates that there is a loss of thirty minutes of time every single month. In addition to this, all of us, as a group, accidentally shut the programme window, which causes us to lose the reports we were working on. If you routinely save your work, you should be able to avoid anything like a one-half hour incident once a month or a one-hour incident like clockwork, which will average out to around one minute for each day. If you do not routinely save your work, you can expect to avoid these incidents.

Individual Who Makes Fun Of Themselves And Says. "I Am In A Very Sedentary State Right Now."

Self-deprecating people often have the misconception that they are incapable of doing a certain task because of their lack of motivation. But since this sort of procrastinator is the complete antithesis of a lazy person, when they don't get anything done, they are more harsh on themselves about it. Sorry, ladies, but this is the kind of business that tends to attract male customers. Instead of recognising that they are genuinely too exhausted to do the task at hand, most people point the blame onto their own stubbornness, laziness, or inactive attitude.

These guys really need to learn to have more compassion for themselves. If you are the sort of person who engages in this kind of procrastination, then the most difficult task for you will be to force yourself to take a break and refresh your mind so that you can tackle the job in an effective manner. Because of the amount of work you have to complete and the impending deadline, you will constantly have the tendency to remark that you do not have much time to relax.

Recharging your own batteries is the approach that you may use to overcome this kind of procrastination so that you can get things done. You may shake off that sensation of lethargy by getting some fresh air and exercise, such as going for a stroll in an open area. This will help you regain the energy that has been depleted from your body.

3. Personality traits of an over booker who declares, "I am quite busy now!"

Do those days on your calendar often seem to be packed with both important events and empty space? If you answered "yes," then you are part of this group. People who overbook their schedules often report feeling overwhelmed as a result of their packed calendar. The well-known phrase "I'm so busy" is likely to be used as an explanation by them rather often.

In the realm of commerce, the individual who is the busy is the one who manages to get the most work done. Nevertheless, the procrastinators who have too many obligations do not fall under this group. They genuinely utilise the fact that they are busy as an excuse for not completing a certain activity. In point of fact, it is not an indicator of activity but rather an evidence of avoidance: rather than tackling the issues head-on, it seems simpler for them to shift the responsibility on having more important things to accomplish.

If you are the sort of person who procrastinates by creating mayhem in order to avoid dealing with a challenging circumstance right immediately, then your greatest obstacle is to realise that this is NOT a job that you need to do. To get over this kind of procrastination, all you need to do is take a step back, give yourself some time, and think about what's going on inside your head. You should make an effort to determine what it is that you are genuinely attempting to keep away from. Finding an answer to that issue will make conquering procrastination a lot simpler for you to do once you have it in your possession.

4. One who is interested in novel experiences and boasts, "I am having the best idea of execution!"

The novelty seeker is the final of our sorts of procrastinators to be discussed. Shiny Object Syndrome is a common condition that affects these kinds of men and women. Such people are continuously coming up with a lot of new ideas to work on, but after a week of working on those projects, they get bored with them. They show a strong interest in the most recent developments in the sector in which they operate, and they are extremely eager to put these developments into practise; but, they do not follow through.

People that engage in this kind of procrastination are also renowned for their ability to take action and make choices with ease. They end up wasting a lot of time and become exhausted, mostly as a consequence of the fact that they do not act consistently in a single direction for a sufficient amount of time to observe the benefits of their efforts.

Make A List Of Things You Need To Do Every Day.

A daily list of activities that you make for yourself to serve as a blueprint for your day is perhaps the most effective tool for time management that you can use.

Every effective manager of time writes down their thoughts and operates from a daily schedule of activities. Effective executives make it a habit to spend a few minutes at the start of each day composing a "to-do" list. This is analogous to the way a pilot goes through a checklist before every takeoff.

The best time to make a list is the night before, so that your subconscious mind may work on your list while you sleep. The best time to make a list is the night before. When you get up in the morning, you will often have "dea" and "nght" that will assist you in achieving some of the most significant goals that are listed on your "lt."

Your preparation for the next day ought to be the very last thing you do at the conclusion of each and every day. In a research that included more than fifty highly successful corporate executives, forty-one of the fifty claimed that the best time management technique they had ever found was a blank pad of paper on which they wrote down everything they needed to accomplish before they started. This was found in a study that involved more than fifty highly effective corporate executives.

Rest more soundly.

During the night, a lot of people toss and turn in an effort to remember something important that they have to do the next day. You will have much better sleep and wake up feeling more refreshed if, before to going to bed, you write down everything that you have planned for the next workday on a list and then construct the list.

Time management experts estimate that writing down a list of the activities you need to do on a given day takes around twelve minutes of your time each day. But the time you spend on this will result in a tenfold increase in the amount of work you get done because to your improved productivity. When you really begin working, an investment of twelve minutes in the preparation of a daily list will result in an increase in productivity equal to one hundred and twenty minutes, or two hours. That is a remarkable reward for such a simple effort.

The ABCDE Method After you have compiled a list of everything that you want to accomplish the next day, the next step is to organise that list by applying the ABCDE method to your activities in the appropriate order.

The word "consequence" is the one that stands out as the most significant in relation to time management.

The significance of a job is determined by the potential repercussions of either completing it or failing to do it. When you are setting priorities, you must apply this approach to each activity, and you must always start with the work that will have the most significant impact on the end result.

In situations like this, the ABCDE method may be quite useful. You should start by writing out everything you need to get done the next day on a list. Then, before you start working, next to each item on your list, write an A, B, C, D, or E.

This should be done before you start working.

You are required to carry out the action indicated by the letter A on the item. It is something that will have really serious repercussions, regardless of whether it is done or not done. Put a 'A' next to the tasks and activities that you have to finish throughout the course of the day in order to complete the responsibilities that have been placed on your shoulders.

Those things that you ought to accomplish are denoted by the letter B. The decision to perform (or not do) B tasks has some minor consequences, but they are not nearly as significant as the decision to do (or not do) A tasks. The golden rule is that you should never do a B activity while there is still an outstanding A activity.

C activities are enjoyable to participate in, but they do not have any consequences, neither positive nor bad. C activities have no impact. Having a friendly conversation with a colleague, grabbing an extra cup of coffee, or checking your email are all things that are nice to do and may be entertaining and pleasurable, but whether or not you choose to engage in these activities has no bearing whatsoever on how well you do your job duties. C activities take up fifty percent of employees' time at work. These are activities that provide no benefit to the company in any way.

Every person is a creature of their own routines. Effective individuals establish positive habits and make them a central focus of their lives. People who are not productive have a tendency to unintentionally establish poor habits, which subsequently come to rule their lives.

Many people get into the routine of arriving at work and immediately engaging in time-wasting activities that provide little to no value once they get there. In most cases, as soon as they arrive, they start feeling better and continue to do so throughout the day. On the other hand, any behaviour you engage in on a regular basis develops into a habit. It is unfortunate that the vast majority of individuals at work today have developed the habit of spending the majority of their time on activities that do not offer anything to their businesses or to their careers. This wastes a lot of time and is not productive in any way. Avoid having this occur to you at all costs.

Delegate as much as you possibly can.

Going back to the ABCDE method, a D activity is something that you are able to hand over to someone else. This is the last step in the method. The rule is that you should delegate all that you can to other people in order to free up more time for you to engage in your A activity. If you follow this rule, you will have more time to devote to your A activity.

Your success in completing your A activities is a major factor that will decide the overall trajectory of your professional life.

An E activity is something that you should completely do away with. After all, the only way you'll be able to get a handle on your time is if you stop doing activities that aren't really necessary for you to accomplish any more.

During the course of their work and career, it is normal and natural for people to fall into a comfort zone. However, it is important for people to push themselves outside of this zone. They get to the point when doing specific activities in a certain manner seems natural to them. Even after being given more levels of responsibility, they continue to take on tasks that aren't actually necessary anymore or that other people are capable of doing just as well as they do or even better. This is despite the fact that they have been promoted to higher levels of responsibility.

Ask yourself, "What would happen if I did not engage in the activity at all?" and think about the consequences of that decision. It is a prime candidate for elimination if it would have a negligible or nonexistent impact on your company or career if you were to get rid of it.

Assessing Productivity While Working To Enhance Our Time Management System

It is essential that you maintain a record of how successful your strategies for managing your time are proving to be now that you have started down the path towards more effective time management. Not only will this help you assess your progress and outcomes, but it will also help you identify the areas in which you need to improve. Both of these benefits will come from doing this.

How to determine the Level of Productivity

Given that productivity is a very nebulous concept, attempting to quantify it may be rather challenging.

Nevertheless, you may acquire a solid notion of productivity by following some simple suggestions.

The most accurate approach to gauge your level of productivity is to apply the methods you use to increase your level of productivity to the typical activities you carry out. You are able to make a note of the amount of time that such jobs used to need in the past while you were doing them. Now, using the new tasks for managing time, carry out actions that are comparable and make a note of the amount of time it takes.

When you do the same chores that you normally do, you will find that you are far more productive. This will become immediately apparent to you.

Improving One's Ability to Manage Time

Additionally, there are a variety of tools and applications that can be downloaded into your computer or mobile device and used. These tools will assist you in more effectively managing your time, which will ultimately lead to an increase in your productivity. Some examples of this are as follows:

Todoist is an excellent programme that helps you to manage the things that you need to do, from managing the tasks that need to be achieved at work to managing the chores that need to be performed at the grocery store. This programme is available for download on both desktop computers and mobile devices. It doesn't cost anything to use.

Trello: Another crucial programme that assists you in efficient time management is Trello, which lets you organise your tasks in a list format. Using this programme, you will be able to coordinate efforts with the members of your team and delegate responsibilities to each individual. The tasks may be completed by members of your team, and the results can be uploaded directly to Trello. In addition to that, there is a plethora of additional useful functionality. In addition, the programme has an engaging and user-friendly card interface that is designed to pique the user's attention.

Time Doctor: Time doctor is yet another useful tool that may assist you in managing your time in an effective manner. With the assistance of this programme, you will be able to keep track of the activities that need to be completed as well as the amount of time that is required to complete each activity. In addition to that, using this programme guarantees that not a single second of your time will be thrown away.

An Appeal to Take Action

Choose any two of the actions that you carry out on a regular basis and carry them out in the typical way. Now, be sure to complete them the next day with the method of time management that we have recommended. Take some notes on how long it takes you to do each of these things on a daily basis. Make your own observations on the time difference.

Increased Productivity And Achievement Are Obtained

It's possible to accomplish a lot while yet falling short of your goals. It is conceivable to do one action to the highest possible standard and get the greatest possible outcomes, while simultaneously failing to perform other activities that would have brought you closer to achieving your objectives. If this occurs, you won't be able to accomplish either your short-term or your long-term objectives.

Good management of one's time is one of the most important factors in one's ability to be successful and productive. Your ability to effectively manage your time enables you to take charge of your life, organise your time, and prioritise your responsibilities in line with the amount of time required to complete each activity.

When you are able to successfully manage your time, you acquire the capacity to attend to all of your daily tasks with the greatest concentration they demand. This guarantees that you generate the best outcomes possible and that you are able to accomplish your objectives.

Employers will come to you when they need additional work done well and in a particular timeframe since they know of your capacity to generate excellent results. If you are a successful employee who completes job on time, they will come to you when they need to get more work done in a specific period. This will enhance the amount of exposure you get in your job, which might lead to promotions.

Sixth Tip: Get More Done in Less Time and with Less Effort

When you design a timetable that directs the time you spend on any given task—which is the very essence of efficient time management—you are able to achieve more while expending less effort and spending less time overall.

You have the capacity to concentrate on one activity at a time rather than multitasking because you have a plan that outlines what you want to accomplish, how you intend to do it, and the amount of time you expect to spend doing it. This increases the likelihood that you will complete all activities or tasks in a shorter amount of time. This in no way indicates that the quality of the job you do will suffer in any way. In point of fact, the fact that you have a strategy will allow for an enormous improvement in the quality of the job you do.

7: Expanded Possibilities for Academic Accomplishment

Learning is an ongoing process that never stops. The more knowledge you have, the more useful you are to others. There is always an opportunity to learn something new. If you take the time to plan, organise, and manage your schedule, you will be able to accomplish all of your daily objectives and still have time left over to take advantage of any educational opportunities.

You may make the most of such chances by doing research on a topic that you believe you need further knowledge on, by attending courses on a part-time basis, and by assisting colleagues or classmates with projects from which you will gain new abilities.

8: Increased Capacity for Adaptability and Spontaneity

When you have solid habits for managing your time, you have the capacity to fit in unplanned activities and make impromptu adjustments to your calendar when the need arises. This gives you the flexibility to respond quickly to changing circumstances.

You will be able to react to any "emergency" quickly and at any time without leaving key daily activities unattended because you will easily be able to rearrange your activities or fit in any significant unanticipated activity into your excess time. This will allow you to respond to any "emergency" without having to leave vital daily tasks unattended. You will not whine about how you did not have enough time to do the things you had planned, nor will you point the finger of blame at the unanticipated activity.

9: Spend More Time on the Things That Really Matter

Managing your time effectively means focusing your efforts on the elements of your life that will have the most influence. If you are able to efficiently manage your time, you will not have to hurry through the things that are important to you because you will have enough time to devote to doing those things.

10: A Life Full of Joy and Good Health

If you learn to manage your time well, you won't have to whine about how you don't have enough hours in the day to do all of the things you need to do. Because every second, minute, and hour of your day will be fully accounted for and planned for, you will find that you are able to take pleasure in your life. You will have complete control over your life and sufficient time to cope with everything and everything that may come your way.

You have a tendency to skip meals or stay up late attempting to accomplish your assignment when you feel as if you are running out of time or when you feel stressed by an activity. This is especially true if the activity is making you feel anxious. This has an effect on your health since it causes your body to degrade when it does not get enough rest or the energy it needs to make it through the day.

If you manage your time, organise your activities, and stick to your schedule, you will be able to achieve all of your objectives on time and your life will run smoothly. This is the perfect formula for a life that is filled with joy, good health, and financial success.

What About The Investigations? How Am I Supposed To Establish A Time Limit When There Is So Much For Me To Discover?

You should prioritise setting a time limit for your study above all other tasks.

In this day and age, when everyone has access to the Internet, it is easy to get carried away with research and get up on Nowhere Island.

You understand what I am getting at. You would not be unfamiliar with this circumstance. You may spend hours attempting to hunt for the most useful knowledge that's already out there, all in the sake of discovering new possibilities.

Trying to locate El Dorado while scouring the Internet for the most reliable information is a futile endeavour.

Therefore, you will establish a time limit in addition to an objective. You should give yourself as little time as possible to do research. Additionally, determine in advance what it is that you want to look into.

Let's say you're working on a piece for your blog on how to avoid becoming distracted. Set a timer for yourself and give yourself just 20 minutes to do research. What, just twenty minutes? If you determine what you need in advance, then the answer is yes, you can do it within that time range. Take, for instance, your decision that you require:

A remark made in the form of a quotation that provokes contemplation.

A recommendation from a credible source to support a claim.

A strategy that a well-known individual employs

You should now be aware that you can spend around seven minutes on each of the items listed above.

To find the quotation, you will just Google "distractions + quotes" and choose the first result that catches your attention.

You will get the authoritative quotation by Googling your comment, which reads as follows: "The best way to beat distractions is to schedule a time for them after you've completed your task."

You look for an article on entrepreneur.com and decide to

paraphrase the author on a remark that is quite close to your own.

Regarding the method, you may find it by Googling "famous people + Pomodoro technique."

You find out that Francesco Cirillo, an Italian, created the Pomodoro method, which is used by 2 million individuals throughout the world. Eugene Scwartz made advantage of it. Before beginning any assignment, he would set the timer for 33.33 minutes and then go to work.

That completes the required amount of information for your article. You managed to get out of the rabbit hole. It could even take you less than twenty minutes, but that is determined on the information that you are looking for.

You now understand how setting a cut-off point for an activity might help you accomplish more. Therefore, make sure that you establish a cut-off point for every item of work that you do without thinking about whether or not you will reach the goal.

Before I let you go, I just want to remind you that you should never begin a project without first setting a deadline.

Work out.

Consider picking up a project you put aside in the past but should have finished because you were too overwhelmed or lost yourself in a rabbit hole.

Put a deadline on it that you can easily meet.

Let's say you've given up on writing a short narrative. Set a timer for five minutes and force yourself to write the following paragraph.

When the timer goes off, you must come to a halt. If you have the want to write more, jot down some notes on what's coming up next.

Attendance the next day is required to proceed.

"A writer whose skill is improved by a deadline: the more time he has, the worse he writes." [Case study] "A writer whose skill is improved by a deadline."

The Most Effective Practises For Organisation

Organisation is one of the most critical factors that determines how productive an individual is. People who are most successful are aware of the fact that it is possible to recover large amounts of time just by organising one's time and space. This time may then be utilised to do more than one could have ever believed possible. In addition, if you organise your surroundings as well as your schedule, you may reduce the tension and anxiety that are caused by the clutter and disorder in your life, which will result in an overall improvement in the quality of your life. In this chapter, you will learn several tried-and-true routines that will assist you in organising your life like a seasoned professional.

The twenty-first routine is to simplify your life.

Your life has to be decluttered before you can even begin to think about organising it. The vast majority of individuals erroneously believe that possessing more goods would result in greater levels of happiness. The exact reverse has been shown to be the case, which is quite disappointing. The plain and basic truth is that the more things there are in your life, whether it be stuff in your workstation or activities in your day, the more tension and anxiety you will experience. In light of this, it is imperative that you simplify your life in each and every manner that is feasible.

A good rule of thumb to follow when determining if an item constitutes clutter in your home is to ask yourself whether you use it on a daily or weekly basis. If you remove that item from a table, drawer or closet, you will liberate space that you can use for something that is more essential, or you can simply leave the area open, creating an atmosphere that is calmer and less crowded. Simply simply, you should look through all of the spaces that you have and get rid of the stuff that you do not use. That is the first step towards organising your life, and it is one of the most crucial steps.

Habit 22: assign Homes for Everything
After you have cleared away the excess stuff, the following step is to assign homes for the things that have been retained in your collection. This will reduce the chaos that you have to pick through while searching for items that don't have a definite place for them, allowing you to find what you need much more quickly. It will also save you

significant time since it will enable you to rapidly get your hands on any item, tool, or accessory that you need simply by enabling you to walk directly to the location where that particular object is stored. It goes without saying that the five minutes you save here and the fact that you now know where everything is will add up to provide you more time that you can put towards the job at hand.

You may take it a step further by using devices such as drawer organisers, desk organisers, and other similar items meant to assist in preventing objects from being jumbled up in a heap. These items are reasonably priced and will provide a feeling of order to any location, even random drawers or other areas that were previously disorganised and frustrating. Your life will become less chaotic and more directed towards fulfilling your goals the more organised your surroundings are.

23rd Routine: Get Your Time in Order

When left to its own devices, time, like space, has the potential to become disorganised, chaotic, and unpleasant. Consequently, in the same way that you clean up and organise your physical area, you should also clean up and organise the way you spend your time. The first thing you need to do is examine your routine and see if there are any tasks, big or little, that can be crossed off the list. This will lighten the weight on your schedule, which will make you feel less stressed about the fact that you have too much to accomplish at any particular moment.

After you have cleaned up the clutter, the next step is to devise a plan for each day of the week. You may not have complete control over how you spend your time at work, but you can devise a productive routine for the time you spend at home, which will enable you to be more productive with the time you have available. You may finally start making progress towards achieving success if you increase the amount of work you get done and decrease the amount of time you spend on things that are a waste of your time.

Focusing on one thing at a time is the twenty-fourth habit.

The last stage in getting your life in order is to organise your thoughts and memories. Getting into the habit of concentrating on one item at a time is the most efficient way to accomplish this goal. The majority of people have the misconception that multitasking is the best approach to get more done in a shorter amount of time. Sadly, a large number of studies have shown that this assertion is not even remotely accurate. The ability to multitask does not make a person more productive; rather, it makes them less productive, decreasing the quantity and quality of the products they produce while simultaneously raising their total stress and anxiety levels.

The key is to keep your attention on just one subject at a time. When you get started on a project, you should see it through to the end before moving on to another one. In the same way, concentrate all of your thoughts and efforts on the one job that you are now working on. Keep your attention on what you're doing rather than letting it stray to other things that could be happening or problems that might be occurring. Your productivity will increase dramatically as a result of this since you will be able to complete a job in a shorter amount of time and with more efficiency.

www.ingramcontent.com/pod-product-compliance
Lightning Source LLC
Chambersburg PA
CBHW050025130526
44590CB00042B/1913